FOLDED FABRIC *Fun*

Nancy J. Martin

An imprint of Martingale & Company

Credits

Photography .... Brent Kane
Illustration and Graphics .... Barb Tourtillotte
Cover Design .... David Chrisman
Text Design .... Judy Petry
Copy Editor .... Liz McGehee

Folded Fabric Fun©

Printed in the United States of America
02 01 00 99 98 12 11 10 9 8

Contents

Introduction

Learning to create handmade projects is always a joy—but we all know that the feeling of accomplishment after completing a project is the greatest reward! With the time constraints so many people have nowadays, the craft of fabric folding can give us that "instant gratification" we often can't get from more time-consuming crafts. And the results are always charming and festive.

The fabric-folding technique consists of just a few simple steps. Fabrics are cut into squares, folded and pressed, then stitched, glued, or fused to a foundation. And the designs you can create from the projects included in this book are truly unlimited.

For Christmas, adorn a length of garland, a wreath, or a tabletop tree with charming folded-fabric ornaments in rich holiday colors. Or create potholders, mug rugs, pillows, tote bags, and purses in the colors of your choice. You can even take the block designs I've included and create your own charming wall hangings. Try using orange and black fabrics to add a wisp of the Halloween spirit to a room, or choose brilliant red, white, and blue hues to salute the Fourth of July with your own "fabric fireworks!" Every design can be altered to fit your imagination, so invent to your heart's content.

Fabric folding is a delightful, enjoyable craft. I hope you get as much satisfaction from making these projects as I have. Now—get ready for some folded fabric fun!

Folded fabric ornaments decorate an evergreen spray hung on a cheery red door.

Upon her return from Thailand, a friend gave me a set of coasters made from a folded star design. The gift inspired me to expand upon this simple, fun technique.

General Directions

Read through the list of materials needed before you begin a craft project. Have all the necessary materials on hand and become familiar with the construction directions before you proceed.

Dimensions, rather than pattern pieces, are given for patterns that are a simple square, rectangle, triangle, or circle. Do not add seam allowances to these measurements; they are already included. Cut pieces the exact size given.

Examine photographs and illustrations to see what an item looks like when completed.

Supplies

Fabric. To achieve a traditional look for these Christmas items, we used a variety of red and green fabrics. For all projects in this book, yardage and requirements specify the amount and type of fabric, and in many cases, color recommendations. You can vary the fabric and color to match your decor, adding creative variations. Yardage amounts are based on 44″–45″ wide fabric. Preshrink and press fabrics before cutting.

In many cases, you will need only a scrap of fabric for your projects. You may use any suitable scrap of fabric that you have. Our materials lists, in some cases, indicate that ⅛ yd. of fabric is necessary because that is the least amount of fabric you can buy. You can expect to have fabric left over.

Thread. For strength and durability, use a good-quality thread, such as cotton-wrapped polyester or cotton. Carefully match thread colors to fabric.

Batting and Stuffing. Polyester stuffing is recommended for projects requiring stuffing. It is available wherever fabric is sold. Several layers of batting are used to pad some of the potholders, the purse, and the tote. A sturdy batting such as needlepunch is preferred.

Rotary Cutter, Mat, and Bias Square™. A rotary cutter and mat will save a great deal of time in cutting strips and bias for binding. The Bias Square™ is the perfect tool to measure and cut small pieces of fabric, such as those needed for the ornaments.

Wonder-Under™. Wonder-Under is a bonding agent for fabric, with adhesive on both sides. Using an iron to apply heat and pressure results in a permanent bond. Refer to manufacturer's directions for best results.

Glue Stick. An ordinary glue stick can be used for constructing folded ornaments. The bond is not permanent, so it will not withstand washing.

Needles and Pins. Betweens or #8 or #9 quilting needles are suitable for all hand sewing. Use only sharp pins on sheer fabric and be careful not to snag fabric. Use a strong, sharp sewing-machine needle (size 12) to stitch through several thicknesses of fabric.

Basic Fabric Folds

Fold strip in half lengthwise.

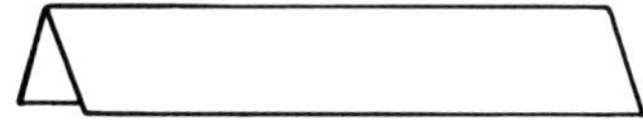

Fold square in half diagonally.

 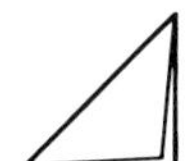

Fold square into quarters.

Fold square into triangle.

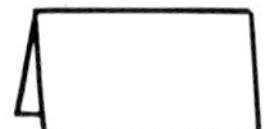 

Assembly Techniques

Note: All directions are written using the word secure. To secure the fabric, you may use any of these four techniques to construct folded fabric ornaments: hand sewing, machine sewing, glue stick, or Wonder-Under™.

Hand Sewing

1. Cut and press folds into all necessary pieces. Divide and label folded fabric according to the row it is used in.
2. Baste background fabric to foundation.
3. Baste Row 1 folded fabric in position. Use a long, sharp needle and be sure to keep basting stitches within ¼″ of edge. When you have finished basting Row 1, knot thread, but do not cut it.

Baste

4. Baste the remaining rows or layers, knotting but not breaking thread after each row. Knot thread firmly after securing final row.
5. Using matching thread, tack down all fabric points.
6. To securely attach all layers, machine stitch close to outside edges within ¼″ seam allowance.
7. Add backing and bind with the finishing technique of your choice.

Machine Sewing

A technique called "chain piecing" allows you to piece a number of ornaments, assembly-line fashion.

1. Prepare strips necessary for ornaments. Cut strip the correct width and a length long enough to make four ornaments, plus an additional inch. Do not cut strip apart into individual segments. Press strip into a lengthwise fold.
2. Cut and press folds into all remaining pieces needed to make four ornaments. Divide and label folded fabric according to the row it is used in.
3. Machine baste each piece of background fabric to a piece of foundation fabric.
4. Place Row 1 strip on four pieces of background and foundation fabric and chain piece. Do not lift presser foot or break thread between pieces; stitch in a long continuous strip. Cut apart into four pieces. Repeat procedure for any remaining strips used in Row 1.

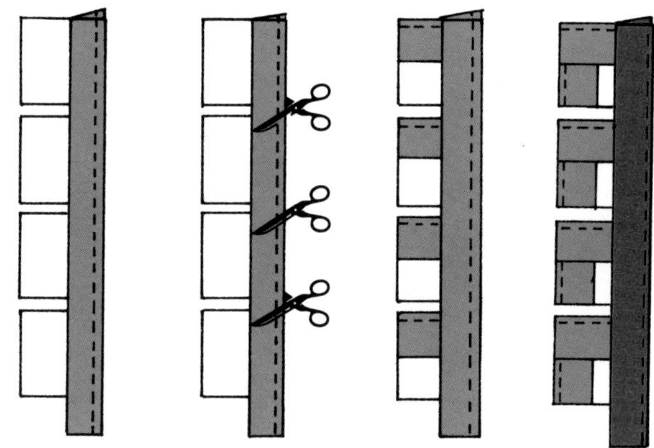

5. Machine stitch all Row 2 strips or squares together assembly-line fashion, working on one side of the block at a time. Cut apart into four pieces.

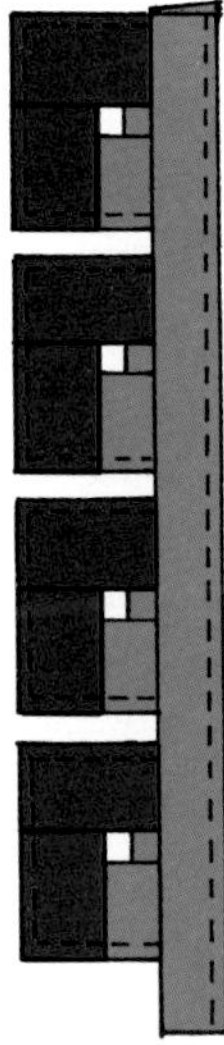

6. Machine stitch the remaining rows or layers.
7. Using matching thread, tack down all fabric points by hand.
8. Add backing and bind with the finishing technique of your choice.

Glue Stick

1. Cut and press folds into all necessary pieces. Divide and label folded fabric according to the row it is used in.
2. Glue background fabric to foundation.
3. Glue Row 1 folded fabric in position on background fabric. Cover entire back side of fabric with glue. Glue may also be used to secure folds that tend to "pop up."

4. Glue remaining rows or layers in the same manner.
5. Glue down the fabric points that need securing.
6. To securely attach all layers, machine stitch close to outside edges within ¼″ seam allowance.
7. Let glue dry; add backing and binding with the finishing technique of your choice.

Wonder-Under™

Lower your ironing board and pull up a chair, for this technique has the advantage of being almost entirely constructed with an iron.

1. Cut Wonder-Under™ into ½″ wide strips.
2. Cut and press folds into all necessary pieces. Divide and label fabric according to the row it is used in.
3. Press Wonder-Under™ to foundation fabric. Remove paper backing. Press background fabric to foundation fabric.
4. Press Wonder-Under™ to back side of Row 1 pieces. Remove paper backing. Press fabric into position on background fabric.
5. Attach the remaining rows or layers in the same manner.
6. Using matching thread, tack down all fabric points.
7. To securely attach all layers, machine stitch close to outside edges within ¼″ seam allowance.
8. Add backing and bind with the finishing technique of your choice.

Finishing Techniques

Narrow Bias Binding

Shown on Log Cabin ornament, page 11

MATERIALS: 45″ wide fabric
3½″ x 3½″ ornament requires 18″ of 1¾″-wide binding
4″ x 4″ ornament requires 20″
7″ x 7″ potholder requires 32″
8″ x 8″ potholder requires 36″

DIRECTIONS

1. Using a rotary cutter and mat, cut 1¾″-wide strips along the bias. Press in half, with wrong sides together and raw edges even. This creates a "double binding."

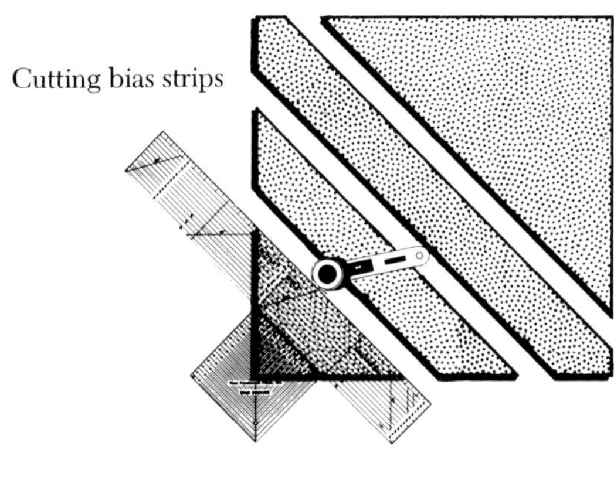

2. Begin at upper corner and use a ¼″ seam allowance. Sew the binding strips to the front of the project through all layers. Stitch until you reach the seam-line point at the corner. Backstitch; cut threads.
3. Turn project to prepare for sewing along the next edge. Fold the binding away from the project, as shown, then fold again to place binding along edge of project. (This fold creates an angled pleat at the corner.)

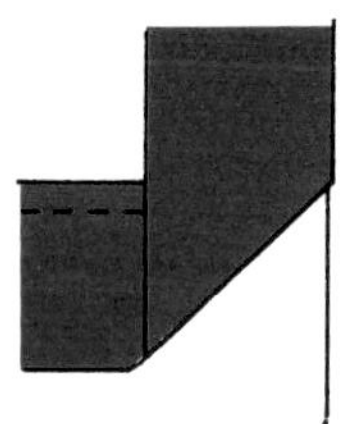

4. Stitch from the fold of the binding to the seam line of the adjacent edge. Backstitch; cut threads. Fold binding as in step 2 and continue around edge.
5. When you reach the top edge of the project, backtack to secure stitching. For potholders, trim binding so it extends 3½″ beyond top of project. This may be omitted for ornaments, which can be hung with hooks, and mug rugs.
6. Turn binding to the back side and blindstitch folded edge in place along previous seam line. At each corner, fold binding in the sequence shown to form a miter on the back of project.

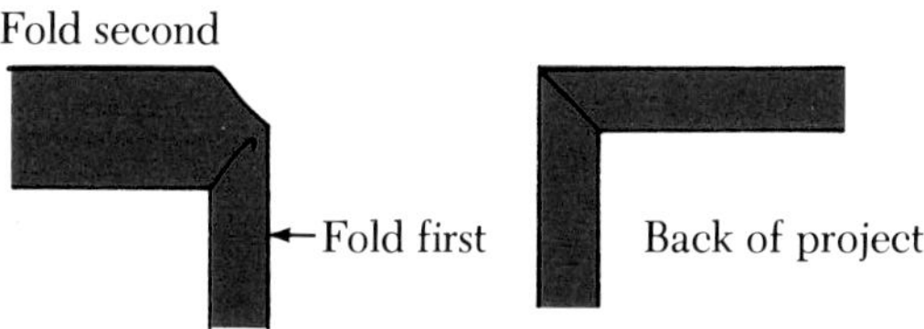

7. For potholders, stitch together raw edges of excess binding. Fold to form a loop and tack in place. Potholder can also be hung by tacking a small plastic or metal ring in one corner.

Fold-Over Binding

Shown on Tree Ornament, page 14.

This technique requires you to cut a backing larger than the front, then fold the edges over to the front to form a false binding.

1. Cut backing 1″ larger than the completed project front.
2. Pin backing behind front, wrong sides together, and baste layers ¼″ from cut edge of project front to keep from shifting.
3. First fold the corner of the backing over the point of the project front. The fold will be touching the corner.

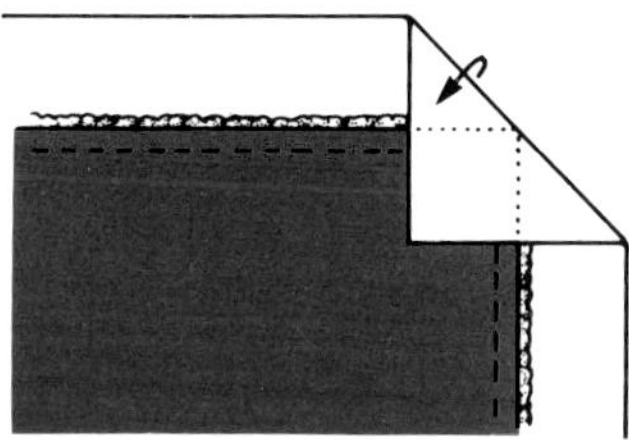

4. Fold the sides of the backing around to the front, folding raw edge to inside.

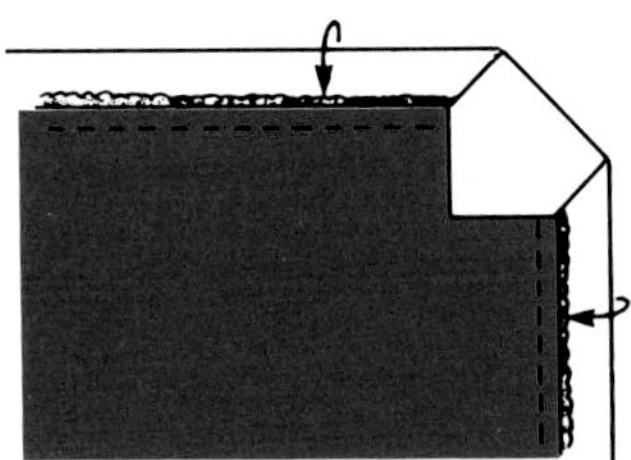

5. Trim away the small square that extends into the corner.

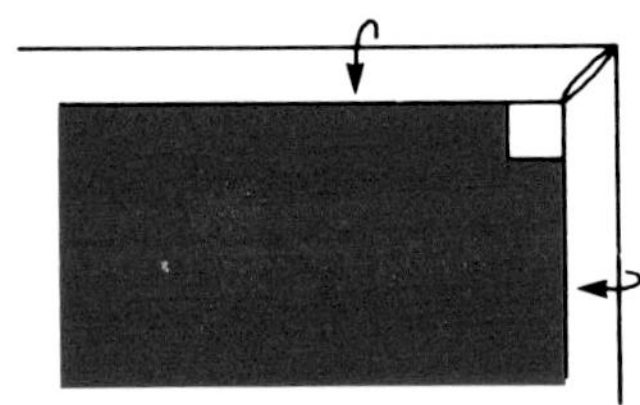

6. Pin folded "binding" in place, then secure with hand or machine stitching.

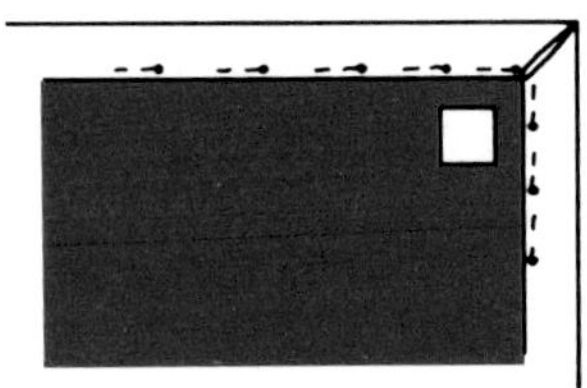

Rick Rack Edging

Shown on Spiral Ornament, page 16.

MATERIALS
3½″ x 3½″ ornament requires 18″ rick rack
4″ x 4″ ornament requires 20″
7″ x 7″ potholder requires 32″
8″ x 8″ potholder requires 36″
Glue stick

DIRECTIONS
1. Trim finished edges clean, ⅛″ beyond seam allowance.
2. Use glue stick to attach rick rack to front edges, matching points of rick rack at corners.
3. Trim rick rack so that it extends 3½″ beyond top of project. Fold rick rack back and tack in place to form a loop.
4. For potholder, you may wish to glue another row of rick rack to the back edges, matching points of rick rack.

Lace Edging

Fan Ornament with lace edging

MATERIALS
3½″ x 3½″ ornament requires 18″ flat lace
4″ x 4″ ornament requires 20″
7″ x 7″ potholder requires 32″
8″ x 8″ potholder requires 36″
Glue stick or Aleene's Tacky Glue
¼ yd. ¼″-wide ribbon or small ring

DIRECTIONS
1. Trim finished edges clean, ⅛″ beyond seam allowance.
2. Beginning in top corner, use glue stick or Aleene's Tacky Glue to attach lace to front edges, folding lace carefully at corners.
3. Tie ribbon into bow; glue to top corner of ornament.
4. For ornament, place hook through lace to hang.
5. For potholder, you may wish to glue another row of lace to the back edges. Tack a small plastic or metal ring in one corner for hanging.

Overcast Edges

Shoo Fly Ornament with overcast edges

DIRECTIONS

1. Use bulky thread and a serger to overcast an edge finish.
2. Hang ornaments with a hook.
3. For potholders, do not snip thread at end of serging, but allow extra thread to fashion a loop for hanging.

Grosgrain Ribbon Edging

Tall Tree Ornament

MATERIALS

3½″ x 3½″ ornament requires 18″ 1″-wide ribbon
4″ x 4″ ornament requires 20″
7″ x 7″ potholder requires 32″
8″ x 8″ potholder requires 36″
Wonder-Under™

DIRECTIONS

1. Cut Wonder-Under™ into a strip ½″ wide by required length. Fuse with iron to one side of ribbon. Press in half lengthwise.
2. Remove paper backing and fuse around edges of ornament.
3. Clip corners so that a miter is formed.

Folded Fabric Ornaments

Folded fabric ornaments (clockwise from top): Stocking, Tree, Diamond-in-a-Square, Shoo Fly, Log Cabin, Christmas Cross, Basket, Folded Radiant Star, and Variable Star in center

Folded Radiant Star Ornament

Folded Radiant Star Ornament

FINISHED SIZE: 3½″ x 3½″

MATERIALS

3½″ x 3½″ square: 1 muslin for foundation
2½″ x 2½″ squares: 5 red for Row 1
3½″ x 3½″ squares: 8 green for Row 2
3½″ x 3½″ squares: 8 white for Row 3
3½″ x 3½″ square: 1 for backing
Finishing material (see pages 7–9)

DIRECTIONS

1. Reserve one of the red 2½″ squares to be used as the star's center. Press all remaining squares as illustrated.

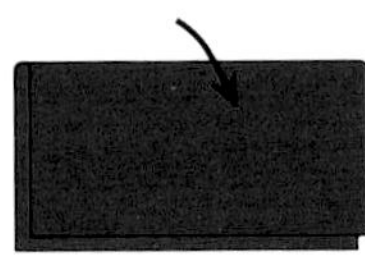
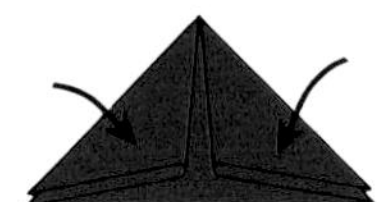

2. Place unpressed 2½″ square in center of 3½″ muslin square. You may wish to secure this with fusible webbing. Position the pressed 2½″ squares as illustrated to form star's center.

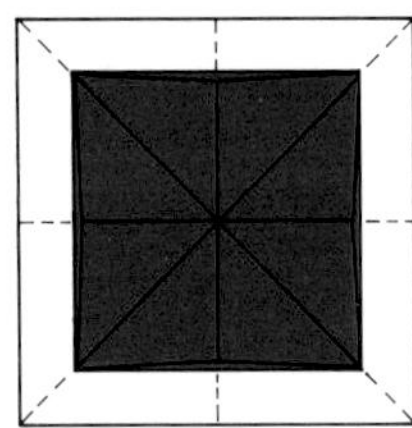

3. Tack these points tightly in place at the star's center. Secure around the outside edges.
4. For the second row of the folded radiant star, place pressed squares as indicated in diagram. They should be ⅜″ from center of fold in the first row. Tack center points in place through all thicknesses. Hand or machine baste around edges to hold in place.

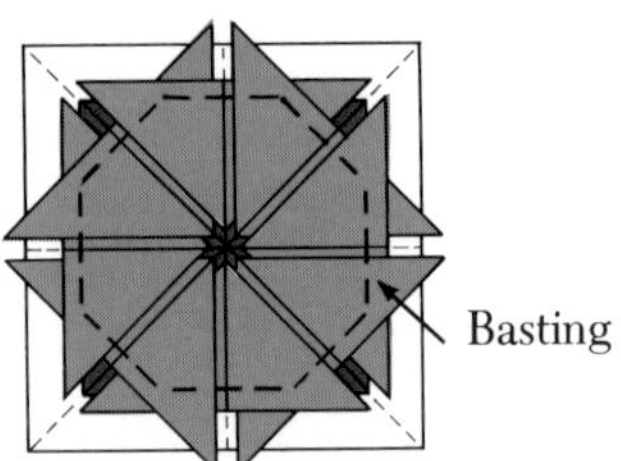

5. Continue in same manner for Row 3. Using foundation fabric as a guide, trim away excess fabric.

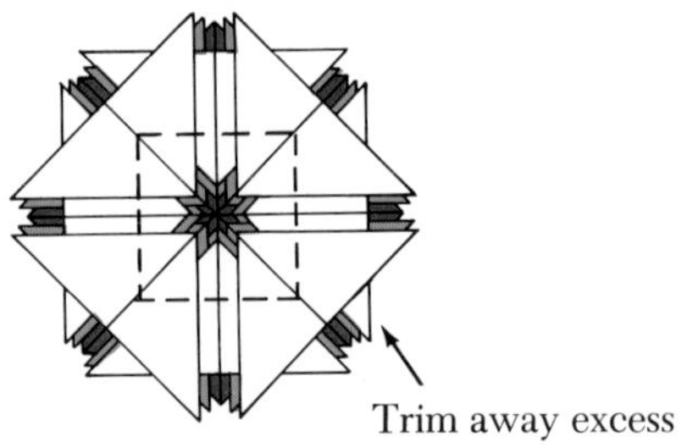

6. Add backing, then use the technique you prefer to finish raw edges (see pages 7–9).

Log Cabin Ornament

Log Cabin Ornament

FINISHED SIZE: 4″ x 4″

MATERIALS

4″ x 4″ square: 1 muslin for foundation
4″ x 4″ square: 1 light background
3½″ x 4″ strips: 2 red print #1, 2 green print #1
2½″ x 4″ strips: 2 red print #2, 2 green print #2
1½″ x 4″ strips: 2 red print #3, 2 green print #3
4″ x 4″ square: 1 for backing
Finishing material (see pages 7–9)

DIRECTIONS

1. Secure light background fabric to foundation.
2. Fold 3½″ x 4″ strips in half lengthwise; press. Place around outside edge of foundation, having fold toward center and raw edges along the outside. Place green strips on 2 adjacent sides of block and red strips on remaining sides. Secure around outside edge.
3. Fold 2½″ x 4″ strips in half; press. Repeat placement given in Step 2; secure.
4. Fold 1½″ x 4″ strips in half; press. Repeat placement given in Step 2; secure.

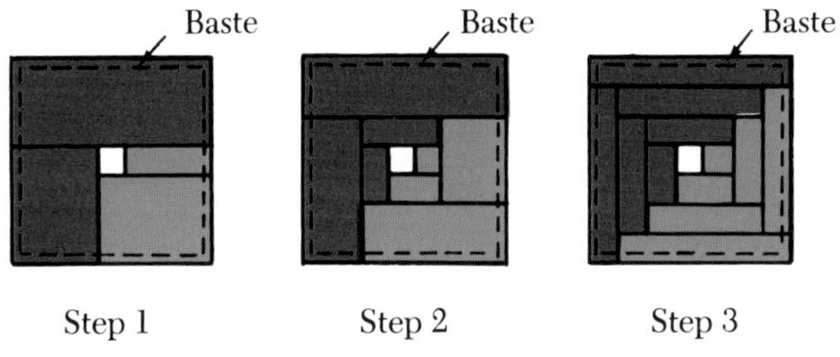

5. Add backing; then use the technique you prefer to finish raw edges (see pages 7–9).

Shoo Fly Ornament

Shoo Fly Ornament

FINISHED SIZE: 3½″ x 3½″

MATERIALS

3½″ x 3½″ square: 1 red for foundation
2½″ x 3½″ strips: 4 muslin for Row 1
2½″ x 2½″ squares: 4 red for Row 2
1½″ x 1½″ squares: 4 muslin for Row 3
3½″ x 3½″ square: 1 for backing
Finishing material (see pages 7–9)

DIRECTIONS

1. Fold muslin strips for Row 1 in half lengthwise; press. Position one on each side of foundation, having fold toward center and raw edges along outside. Secure by hand or machine along outside edges.
2. Fold red squares for Row 2 into quarters; press. Position one square in each corner, having raw edges even; secure. Using red thread, tack points through all layers.
3. Fold muslin squares for Row 3 in half diagonally. Position one in each corner, having raw edges even. Secure along outside edges.

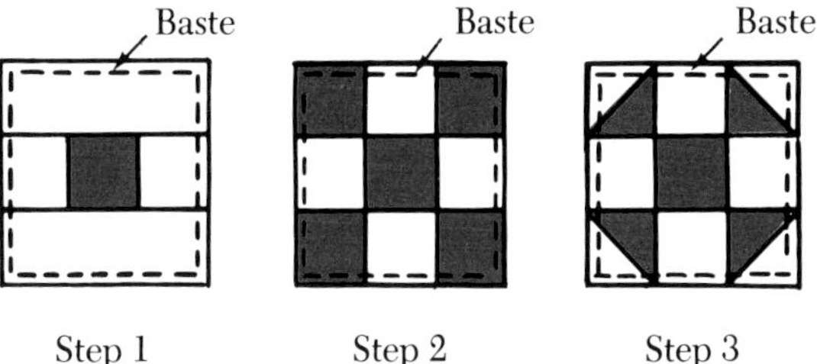

4. Add backing; then use the technique you prefer to finish raw edges (see pages 7–9).

Variable Star Ornament

Variable Star Ornament

FINISHED SIZE: 3½″ x 3½″

MATERIALS

3½″ x 3½″ square: 1 muslin for foundation
3½″ x 3½″ square: 1 red for star center
2¾″ x 2¾″ squares: 4 white for Row 1
2″ x 3½″ strips: 4 green for Row 2
2″ x 2″ squares: 4 white for Row 3
3″ x 3″ squares: 4 white for Row 4
3½″ x 3½″ square: 1 for backing
Finishing material (see pages 7–9)

DIRECTIONS

1. Secure 3½″ red square for star center to foundation.
2. Fold 2¾″ white squares for Row 1 in half diagonally; press. Position one in each corner of foundation, having fold toward center and raw edges along outside. Secure along outside edges.

3. Fold green strips for Row 2 in half lengthwise; press. Position one on each side, having fold toward center and raw edges along outside; secure. Using green thread, tack through all layers at points of red center diamond.

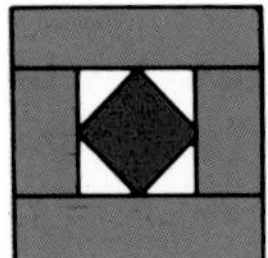

4. Fold 2″ white squares for Row 3 in quarters; press. Position one in each corner, having raw edges even; secure.

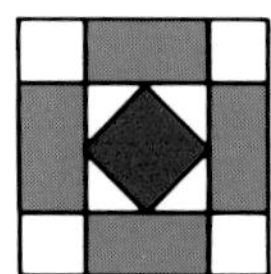

5. Fold 3″ white squares for Row 4 in quarters; press. Position one on each side, aligning point of square with center diamond; secure. Trim away excess.

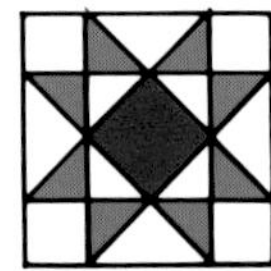

6. Using white thread, tack all points of white squares through all layers.
7. Add backing, then use the technique you prefer to finish raw edges (see pages 7–9).

Stocking Ornament

A teddy bear holds a Stocking Ornament

FINISHED SIZE: 4″ x 5″

MAKES 4 ORNAMENTS

MATERIALS: 45″ wide fabric

¼ yd. muslin
¼ yd. light background fabric
⅛ yd. each of 4 green prints
⅛ yd. each of 4 red prints

White felt
¼ yd. fabric for backing
Bias strip for binding

CUTTING
8″ x 8″ square: 1 muslin for foundation
8″ x 8″ square: 1 light background fabric
4½″ x 8″ strips: 2 green print #1, 2 red print #1
3½″ x 8″ strips: 2 green print #2, 2 red print #2
2½″ x 8″ strips: 2 green print #3, 2 red print #3
1½″ x 8″ strips: 2 green print #4, 2 red print #4
2″ x 12″ strip: 1 white felt
8″ x 8″ square: 1 for backing

DIRECTIONS
1. Baste light background square to foundation.
2. Fold 4½″ x 8″ strips in half lengthwise; press. Place around outside edge of foundation, having fold toward center and raw edges along outside. Place green strips on first two sides of block and red strips on remaining sides. Baste by hand or machine (see Log Cabin ornament on page 11).
3. Fold 3½″ x 8″ strips in half lengthwise; press. Repeat placement given in Step 2; secure.
4. Fold 2½″ x 8″ strips in half lengthwise; press. Repeat placement given in Step 2; secure.
5. Fold 1½″ x 8″ strips in half lengthwise; press. Repeat placement given in Step 2; secure.
6. Cut completed block into quarters. Place stocking pattern, found on page 30, on each quarter and cut out shape.

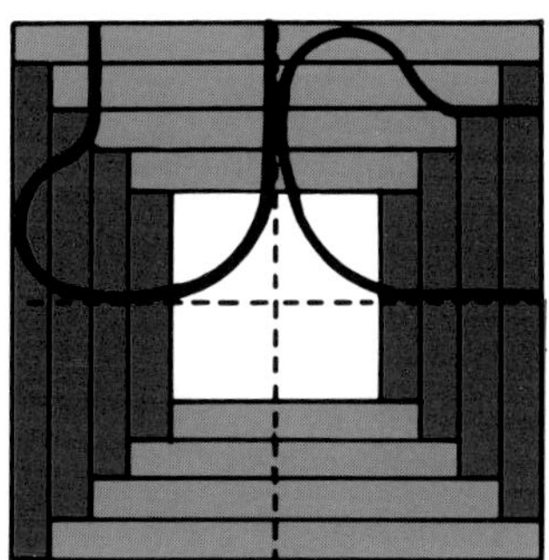

7. Place white felt strip on top of stocking front, having raw edges even; stitch with a ¼″ seam. Fold to inside, forming cuff. Baste raw edge of felt over seam.
8. Using pattern piece as a guide, cut stocking back from fabric. Hem upper edge. Pin to stocking front, wrong sides together; baste.
9. Following directions on page 7, bind with 1¾″ strips of bias fabric. Leave an extra 3″ of bias binding to form loop for hanging at top of stocking. Tack end of binding on back side of stocking, turning under raw edge.

Diamond-in-a-Square Ornament

Diamond-in-a-Square Ornament

FINISHED SIZE: 3½″ x 3½″

MATERIALS
3½″ x 3½″ square: 1 muslin for foundation
2½″ x 3½″ strips: 4 green prints for Row 1
2½″ x 2½″ squares: 4 green prints for Row 2
1½″ x 3½″ strips: 4 green prints for Row 3
1½″ x 1½″ squares: 4 muslin for Row 4
3½″ x 3½″ square: 1 for backing
Finishing material (see pages 7–9)

DIRECTIONS
1. Fold 2½″ x 3½″ green strips for Row 1 in half lengthwise; press. Place around outside edge of foundation, having fold toward center and raw edges along outside; secure.

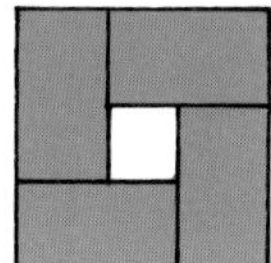

2. Fold green squares for Row 2 in half diagonally; press. Place in each corner of foundation, having fold toward center and raw edges along outside; secure.

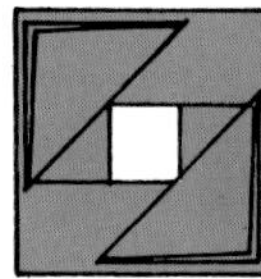

3. Fold 1½" x 3½" green strips for Row 3 in half lengthwise; press. Position and secure as in Step 1.

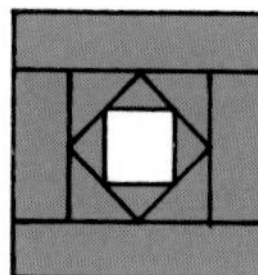

4. Fold muslin squares for Row 4 in half diagonally; press. Position and secure as in Step 2.

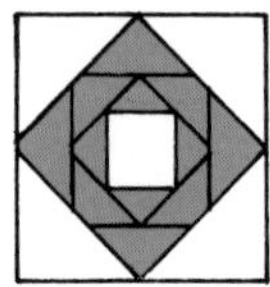

5. Using the technique you prefer, finish raw edges (see pages 7–9).

Tree Ornament

Tree Ornament

FINISHED SIZE: 3½"x 3½"

MATERIALS

3½" x 3½" square: 1 muslin for foundation
1½" x 3½" strip: 1 brown for trunk
4½" x 7" strip: 1 green print #1
3½" x 7" strip: 1 green print #2
2½" x 7" strip: 1 green print #3
1½" x 7" strip: 1 green print #4
3½" x 3½" square: 1 for backing
Finishing material (see pages 7–9)

DIRECTIONS

1. Fold brown fabric for trunk into thirds lengthwise; press. Position trunk on foundation fabric and pin in place.
2. Fold green print #1 in half lengthwise; press. Cut in half. Position these strips on foundation 1¼" from bottom, having fold toward trunk and raw edges toward upper corner; secure.

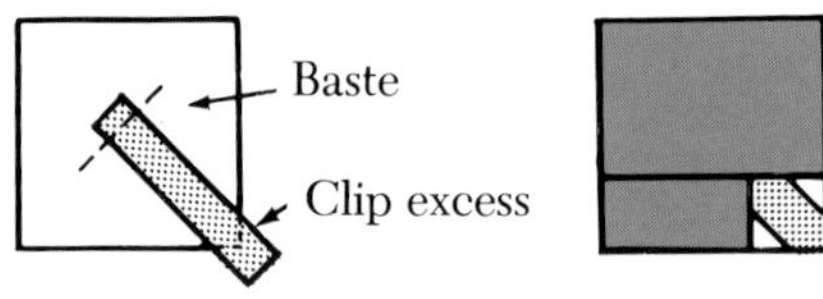

3. Fold, press, and cut apart green prints #2, #3, and #4 in the same manner, positioning strips ½" apart. Secure after positioning each row.

4. Add backing, then use the technique you prefer to finish raw edges (see pages 7–9).

Basket Ornament

Basket Ornament

FINISHED SIZE: 3½" x 3½"

MATERIALS

3½" x 3½" square: 1 muslin for foundation
4" x 4" square: 1 red for basket
6" lace trim, ½" wide (optional)

1½″ x 7″ strip: 1 red for basket handle
1½″ x 7″ strip: 1 muslin
1½″ x 1½″ squares: 2 red for basket bottom
1¾″ x 1¾″ square: 1 muslin
3½″ x 3½″ square: 1 for backing
Finishing material (see pages 7–9)

DIRECTIONS

1. Fold red square for basket in half diagonally; press. Add optional lace trim, if desired. Place on foundation, having fold toward top and raw edges even. Secure along outside edges. Trim away excess fabric at corners.

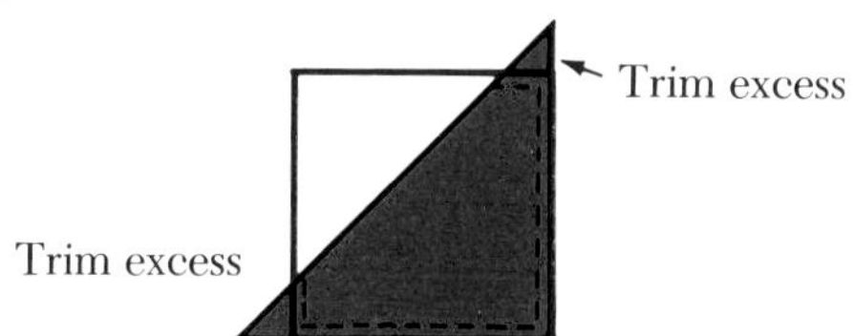

2. Press strip for basket handle into thirds. Press fold at center of strip. Position on foundation, placing raw edges under basket. Tack handle at top center and at folded edge of basket.
3. Fold muslin strip in half lengthwise; press. Cut in half. Position each half along lower sides of ornament, having raw edges even; secure.

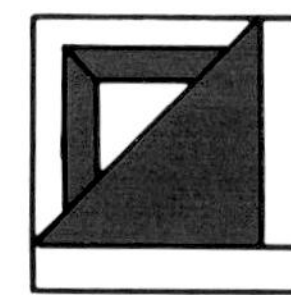

4. Fold 1½″ red squares into quarters; press. Position along lower edge of basket; secure. Tack points.

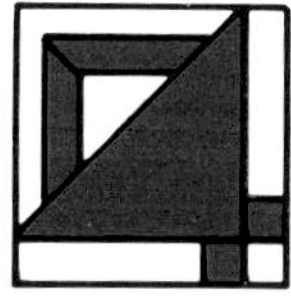

5. Fold muslin square diagonally; press. Position in lower corner, having raw edges even; secure. Tack at corner.

6. Add backing, then use the technique you prefer to finish raw edges (see pages 7–9).

Lace-trimmed Fan Ornaments, Basket Ornaments stuffed with pink baby's breath, and shiny blue Christmas balls create a pastel Christmas decor.

Fan Ornament

Fan Ornament

FINISHED SIZE: 3½″ x 3½″

MATERIALS

3½″ x 3½″ square: 1 muslin for foundation
3½″ x 3½″ square: 1 red for center of fan
3″ x 9″ strips: 3 green prints for fan sides
2″ x 2″ square: 1 red for fan corner
3½″ x 3½″ square: 1 for backing
Finishing material (see pages 7–9)

DIRECTIONS

1. Secure 3½″ red square for center of fan to foundation.
2. Fold green fabrics in half lengthwise; press. Cut each strip in half. Position green strips on foundation, having first strip 1″ from lower corner. Fabric folds should be toward center and raw edges toward the outside. Overlap 3 green strips on each side of fan. Pin; then secure in place. Trim away excess from each strip, using foundation fabric as a guide.

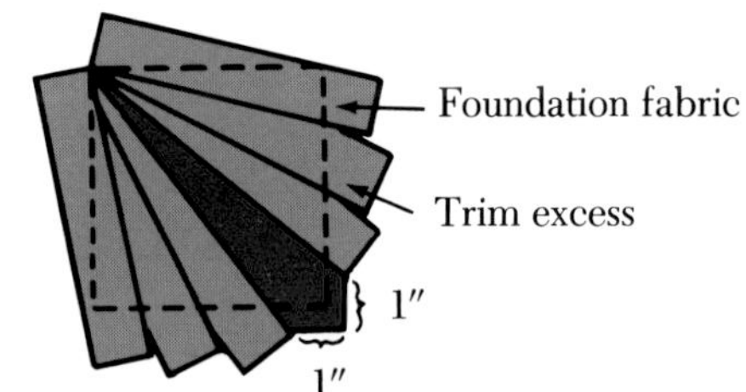

3. Fold 2″ red square into a triangle for corner; secure in place. Tack corner down.
4. Add backing, then use the technique you prefer to finish raw edges (see pages 7–9).

Christmas Cross Ornament

Christmas Cross Ornament

FINISHED SIZE: 3½″ x 3½″

MATERIALS

3½″ x 3½″ square: 1 muslin for foundation
2½″ x 2½″ square: 1 red for star center
2¾″ x 2¾″ squares: 4 white for Row 1
2″ x 3½″ strips: 4 green for Row 2
2″ x 2″ squares: 4 white for Row 3
3½″ x 3½″ square: 1 for backing
Finishing material (see pages 7–9)

DIRECTIONS

1. Secure red square for star center to foundation.
2. Fold 2¾″ white squares for Row 1 in half diagonally; press. Position one in each corner of foundation, having fold toward center and raw edges along outside. Secure along outside edges.

3. Fold green strips for Row 2 in half lengthwise; press. Position one on each side, having fold toward center and raw edges along outside; secure. Using green thread, tack through all layers at points of red center diamond.

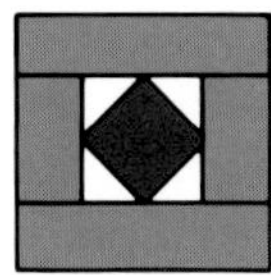

4. Fold 2″ white squares for Row 3 in quarters; press. Position one in each corner, having raw edges even; secure.

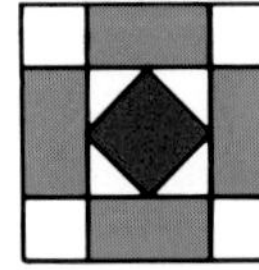

5. Add backing, then use the technique you prefer to finish raw edges (see pages 7–9).

Spiral Ornament

Spiral Ornament

Use striped fabric or sew together fabric strips in Christmas colors to create this lively ornament. Practice this design by first making the potholder on pages 22–23. The strips for the potholder are larger and easier to manipulate while you are learning the technique.

FINISHED SIZE: 4″ x 4″

MATERIALS: 45″ wide fabric
¼ yd. lengthwise striped fabric
4″ x 4″ square: 1 muslin for foundation
4″ x 4″ square: 1 for backing
Finishing material (see pages 7–9)

DIRECTIONS

1. Cut striped fabric into 3 crosswise strips (from selvage to selvage), each 2½″ wide.
2. Press fabric in half lengthwise. You should now have 3 folded strips, each 1¼″ wide.
3. Fold foundation square in quarters; press creases. Fold once again into diagonal quarters; press creases.

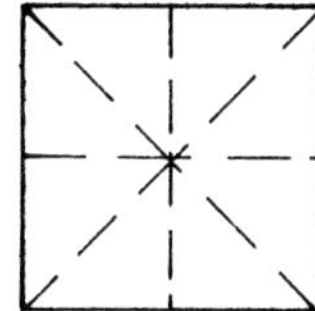

4. Beginning on a diagonal crease, position folded strip, having folded edge on crease and strip extending from center to outside corner. Roughly trim excess. Block will be recut later with a rotary cutter. Secure.

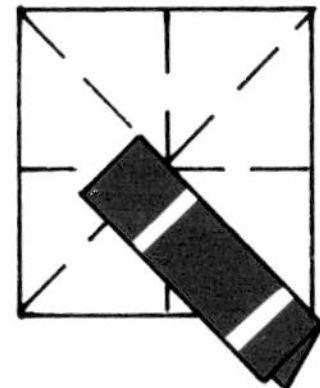

5. Overlap folded strip, placing it evenly between previous strip and next fold. Folded edges should face the same direction and strip should extend from center to outside edge, matching stripes. To match, you may need to trim excess on both ends.

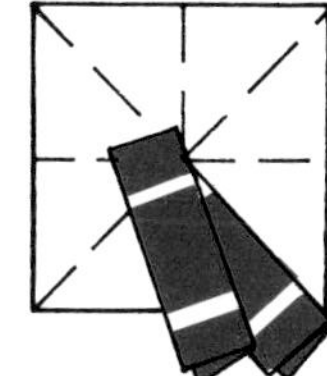

6. Continue overlapping folded strips around foundation, matching stripes and roughly trimming away excess. When you have covered half of the foundation, you will need to tuck in excess strip under previous strip in center. Trim so you are not tucking in too much fabric. Use an awl or long pin to help tuck fabric under. Save all strips that do not "match." You may be able to use them later as spiral moves around foundation.

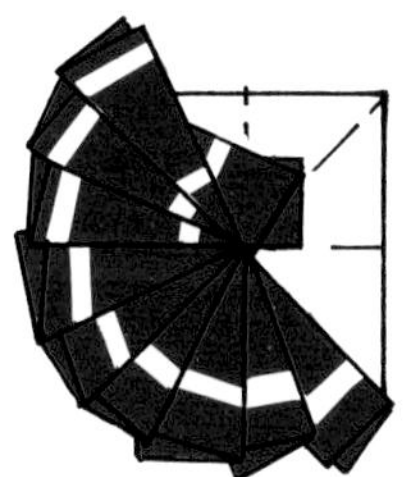

7. Carefully tuck under and secure final strip. Notice that the stripes may not match original strip since the spiral has broadened. Minor adjustments can be made to first strip, but an even match is not necessary to achieve spiral effect.

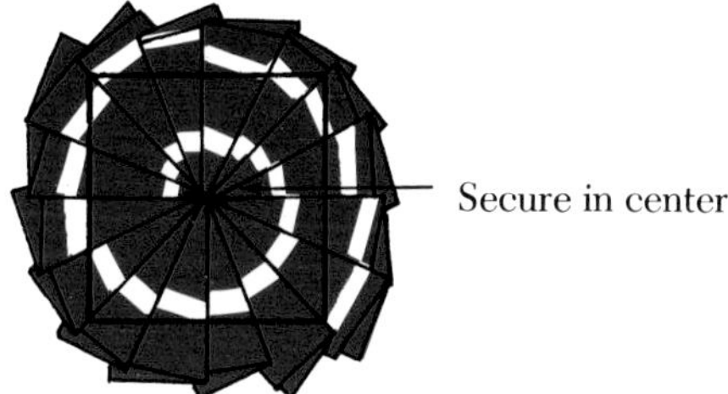

8. Using a machine or hand stitch, tack center securely.

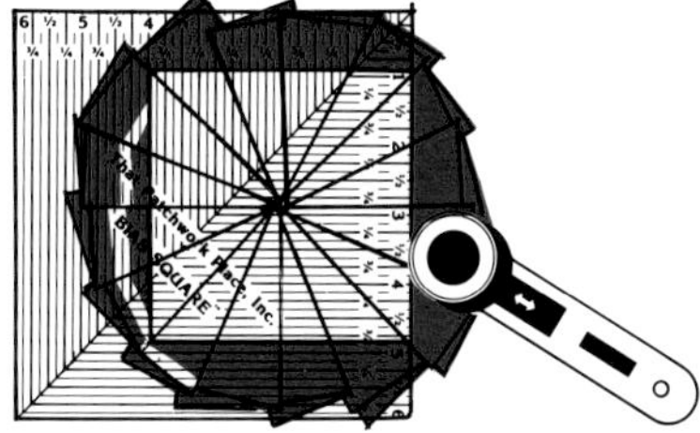

9. Secure around outside edges. Turn spiral ornament to wrong side. Using a rotary cutter and ruler, neatly trim away excess.
10. Add backing, then use the technique you prefer to finish raw edges (see pages 7–9).

Tall Tree Ornament

Tall Tree Ornament

FINISHED SIZE: 2¾″ x 4¼″

MATERIALS

2¾″ x 4¼″ strip: 1 muslin for foundation
2¾″ x 4¼″ strip: 1 green print #1 for center of tree
1½″ x 8″ strips: 1 each of green prints #2, #3, #4
2½″ x 8″ strip: 1 white for outside edge
2″ x 2¾″ strip: 1 dark for ground
2¾″ x 4¼″ strip: 1 for backing
Finishing material (see pages 7–9)

DIRECTIONS

1. Secure green print #1 strip to foundation.
2. Fold remaining green prints in half lengthwise; press. Cut each strip in half. Position green strips on foundation, working from the center toward the outside. Fabric folds should be placed toward the center and raw edges toward outside. Overlap 3 green strips on each side of tree. Pin; then secure in place.

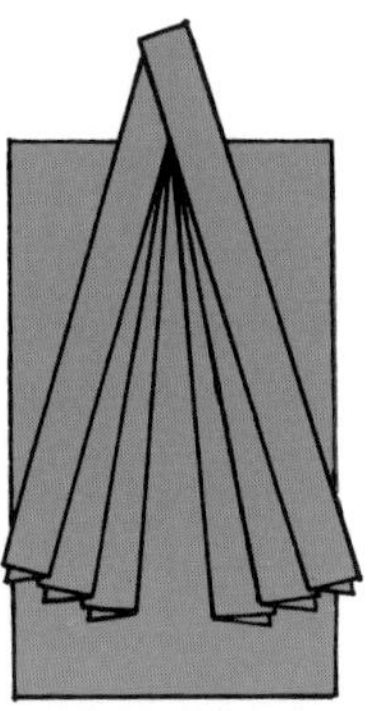

3. Fold white strip in half lengthwise; press. Cut in half. Position along each side of tree to form background.

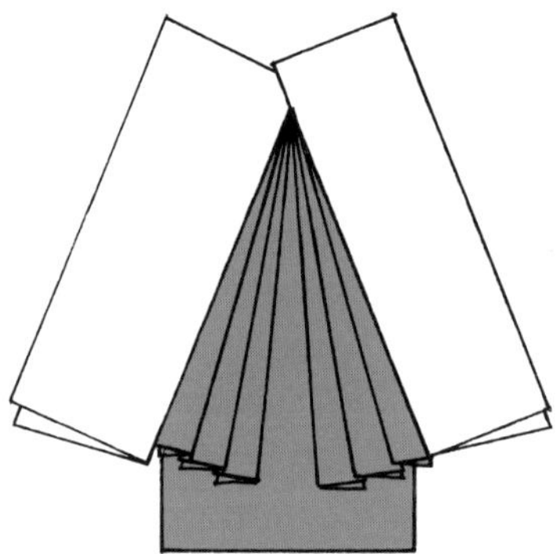

4. Fold dark strip in half lengthwise. Position along bottom of tree.
5. Trim away excess fabric, using foundation fabric as a guide.

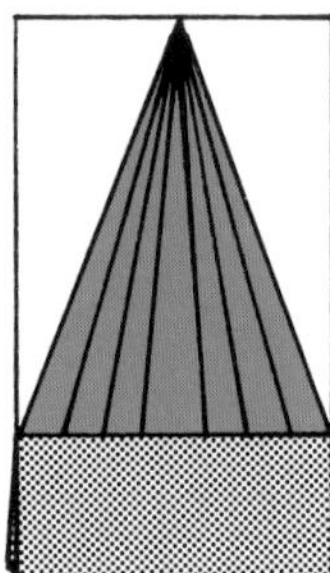

6. Add backing, then use the technique you prefer to finish raw edges (see pages 7–9).

For the Kitchen

By enlarging the ornament designs to 7″ or 8″, you can make potholders. They will serve a useful purpose during the holidays while brightening up your kitchen. Make another set with matching mug rugs and towel top to coordinate with your year-round kitchen decor.

Folded Star Potholder

FINISHED SIZE: 8″ x 8″

MATERIALS: 45″ wide fabric
¼ yd. muslin
⅜ yd. green fabric
⅜ yd. red fabric
¼ yd. fabric for backing
Finishing material (see pages 7–9)

CUTTING
8″ x 8″ square: 1 muslin for foundation
3½″ x 3½″ squares: 5 green for star center and Row 1
3½″ x 3½″ squares: 8 red for Row 2
3½″ x 3½″ squares: 8 green for Row 3
3½″ x 3½″ squares: 16 red for Row 4
3½″ x 3½″ squares: 16 green for Row 5
4½″ x 4½″ squares: 4 red for Row 6
8″ x 8″ square: 1 for backing

DIRECTIONS

1. Reserve one of the 3½″ squares to be used as the star center. Press all remaining squares, except for 4½″ squares, as illustrated.

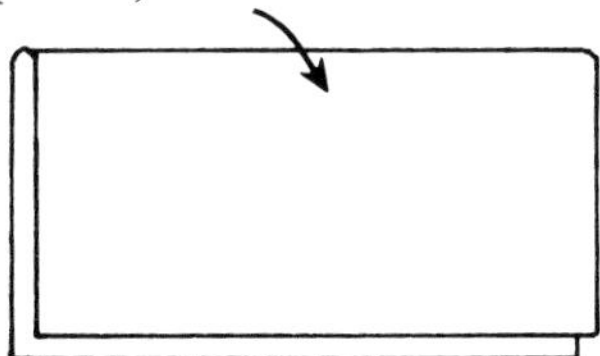

2. Place unpressed 3½″ square in center of 8″ muslin square. You may wish to secure this with fusible webbing. Position the pressed 3½″ squares as illustrated to form star center.

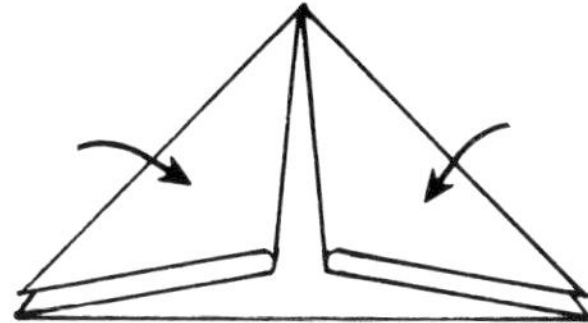

Potholders, Log Cabin Mug Rugs, a kitchen towel with a bright Log Cabin top and a Diamond-in-a-Square Tote Bag brighten this holiday table.

Potholders (left to right): Tree, Folded Star, Christmas Cross, Variable Star, and Spiral done in the 7″ or 8″ size

3. Secure these points tightly in place at star center. Secure outside edges.
4. For the second row of the Folded Radiant Star, place pressed squares as indicated in diagram. They should be ⅜″ from center of fold in the first row. Secure center points in place through all thicknesses. Secure outside edges to hold in place.

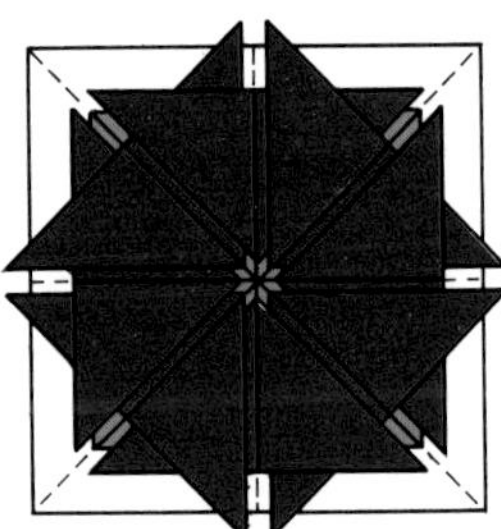

5. Continue in the same manner for rows 3, 4, and 5.
6. Beginning with Row 4, add 2 extra fabric folds to each corner. Continue in the same manner for Row 5.

7. For Row 6, add 4 pressed squares in outer corner. Trim away excess fabric. Completed star will look like this:

8. Add backing fabric. Potholder does not require batting as folded layers of fabric provide sufficient thickness.
9. Using the technique you prefer, finish raw edges (see pages 7–9).

Log Cabin Potholder

FINISHED SIZE: 8″ x 8″

MATERIALS: 45″ wide fabric
¼ yd. muslin
¼ yd. light background fabric
¼ yd. each of red prints #1 and #2
¼ yd. each of green prints #1 and #2
⅛ yd. of red print #3
⅛ yd. of green print #3
Firm batting or needlepunch
¼ yd. fabric for backing
Finishing material (see pages 7–9)

CUTTING
8″ x 8″ square: 1 muslin for foundation
8″ x 8″ square: 1 light background fabric for center
7″ x 8″ strips: 2 red print #1, 2 green print #1
5″ x 8″ strips: 2 red print #2, 2 green print #2
3″ x 8″ strips: 2 red print #3, 2 green print #3
8″ x 8″ squares: 2 firm batting or needlepunch
8″ x 8″ square: 1 for backing

DIRECTIONS
1. Refer to page 11 for construction diagrams.
2. Secure light background fabric to foundation.
3. Fold 7″ x 8″ strips in half lengthwise; after folding they should measure 3½″ x 8″; press. Place around outside edge of foundation, having fold toward center and raw edges along the outside. Place green strips on 2 adjacent sides of block, then overlap red strips on remaining 2 sides. Secure around outside edges.
4. Fold 5″ x 8″ strips in half lengthwise; press. Repeat placement given in Step 2; secure.
5. Fold 3″ x 8″ strips in half lengthwise; press. Repeat placement given in Step 2; secure.
6. Baste 2 layers of batting or needlepunch to one side of folded log cabin. Add backing fabric.
7. Using the technique you prefer, finish raw edges (see pages 7–9).

Variable Star Potholder

FINISHED SIZE: 7″ x 7″

MATERIALS: 45″ wide fabric
¼ yd. muslin
¼ yd. red fabric
⅛ yd. green fabric
⅜ yd. white fabric
Firm batting or needlepunch
¼ yd. fabric for backing
Finishing material (see pages 7–9)

CUTTING
7″ x 7″ square: 1 muslin for foundation
7″ x 7″ square: 1 red for star center
5½″ x 5½″ squares: 4 white for Row 1
4″ x 7″ strips: 4 green for Row 2
4″ x 4″ squares: 4 white for Row 3
6″ x 6″ squares: 4 white for Row 4
7″ x 7″ squares: 2 firm batting or needlepunch
7″ x 7″ square: 1 for backing

DIRECTIONS
1. Refer to page 12 for construction diagrams.
2. Secure red square for star center to foundation.
3. Fold 5½″ white squares for Row 1 in half diagonally; press. Position one square in each corner of foundation, having fold toward center and raw edges along outside. Secure along outside edges.
4. Fold green strips for Row 2 in half lengthwise; press. Position one strip on each side, having fold toward center and raw edges along outside. Baste by hand or machine. Using green thread, tack all points of red center diamond through all layers.
5. Fold 4″ white squares for Row 3 in quarters; press. Position one in each corner, having raw edges even; secure.
6. Fold 6″ white squares for Row 4 in quarters; press. Position one on each side, aligning point of square with center diamond; secure. Trim away excess.
7. Using white thread, tack all points of squares through all layers.
8. Baste 2 layers of batting or needlepunch to one side of folded fabric star. Add backing fabric.
9. Using the technique you prefer, finish raw edges (see pages 7–9).

Tree Potholder

FINISHED SIZE: 7″ x 7″

MATERIALS: 45″ wide fabric
¼ yd. muslin
¼ yd. each of green prints #1, #2, and #3
⅛ yd. of green print #4
Firm battting or needlepunch
¼ yd. fabric for backing
Finishing material (see pages 7–9)

CUTTING
7″ x 7″ square: 1 muslin for foundation
2½″ x 6″ strip: 1 brown for trunk
9″ x 14″ strip: 1 green print #1
7″ x 14″ strip: 1 green print #2
5″ x 14″ strip: 1 green print #3
3″ x 14″ strip: 1 green print #4
8″ x 8″ squares: 2 firm batting or needlepunch
7″ x 7″ square: 1 for backing

DIRECTIONS
1. Refer to page 14 for construction diagrams.
2. Fold brown fabric for trunk into thirds lengthwise; press. Position trunk on foundation fabric; secure. Clip away excess from corner.
3. Fold green print #1 in half lengthwise; press. Cut in half. Position these strips on foundation 3½″ from bottom, having fold toward trunk and raw edges toward upper corner; secure.
4. Fold, press, and cut apart green prints #2, #3, and #4 in the same manner, positioning strips ½″ apart. Secure after positioning each row.
5. Baste 2 layers of batting or needlepunch to one side of folded fabric star. Add backing fabric.
6. Using the technique you prefer, finish raw edges (see pages 7–9).

Fan Potholder

FINISHED SIZE: 7″ x 7″

MATERIALS: 45″ wide fabric
¼ yd. muslin
¼ yd. red fabric
¼ yd. each of 4 green fabrics
Firm batting or needlepunch
¼ yd. fabric for backing
Finishing material (see pages 7–9)

CUTTING
7″ x 7″ square: 1 muslin for foundation
7″ x 7″ square: 1 red for center of fan
6″ x 10″ strips: 2 each of 4 green prints
4″ x 4″ square: 1 red for fan corner
7″ x 7″ squares: 2 firm batting or needlepunch
7″ x 7″ square: 1 for backing

DIRECTIONS
1. Refer to page 16 for construction diagrams.
2. Baste red square for fan to foundation.
3. Fold green prints in half lengthwise; press. Cut each strip in half. Position these strips on foundation, having first strip 2″ from lower corner. Fabric folds should face toward center and raw edges toward outside. Overlap 4 green strips on each side of fan. Pin; then secure in place. Trim away excess from each strip, using foundation fabric as a guide.
4. Fold 4″ red square into a triangle for corner. Trim away excess; secure in place. Tack corner to center of fan.
5. Baste 2 layers of batting or needlepunch to one side of folded fan. Add backing fabric.
6. Using the technique you prefer, finish raw edges (see pages 7–9).

Christmas Cross Potholder

FINISHED SIZE: 7″ x 7″

MATERIALS: 45″ wide fabric
¼ yd. muslin
¼ yd. red fabric
⅜ yd. white fabric
⅛ yd. green fabric
Firm batting or needlepunch
¼ yd. fabric for backing
Finishing material (see pages 7–9)

CUTTING
7″ x 7″ muslin for foundation
7″ x 7″ red square for star center
5½″ x 5½″ squares: 4 white for Row 1
4″ x 7″ strips: 4 green for Row 2
4″ x 4″ squares: 4 white for Row 3
6″ x 6″ squares: 4 white for Row 4
7″ x 7″ squares: 2 firm batting or needlepunch
7″ x 7″ square: 1 for backing

DIRECTIONS
1. Refer to page 16 for construction diagrams.
2. Secure red square for star center to foundation.
3. Fold white squares for Row 1 in half diagonally; press. Position one square in each corner of foundation, having fold toward center and raw edges along outside. Secure along outside edges.
4. Fold green strips for Row 2 in half lengthwise; press. Position one strip on each side, having fold toward center and raw edges along outside. Baste by hand or machine. Using green thread, tack points of red center diamond through all layers.
5. Fold squares for Row 3 in quarters; press. Position one in each corner, having raw edges even; secure.
6. Using white thread, tack points of squares through all layers.
7. Baste 2 layers of batting or needlepunch to one side of folded fabric star. Add backing fabric.
8. Using the technique you prefer, finish raw edges (see pages 7–9).

Spiral Potholder

FINISHED SIZE: 7½″ x 7½″

MATERIALS: 45″ wide fabric
¼ yd. muslin
⅜ yd. lengthwise striped fabric
Firm batting or needlepunch
¼ yd. fabric for backing
Finishing material (see pages 7–9)

CUTTING
7½″ x 7½″ square: 1 muslin for foundation
7½″ x 7½″ squares: 2 firm batting or needlepunch
7½″ x 7½″ square: 1 for backing

DIRECTIONS

1. Refer to page 17 for construction diagrams.
2. Cut striped fabric into 3 crosswise strips (from selvage to selvage), each 3½″ wide.
3. Press fabric in half lengthwise. You should now have 3 folded strips, each 1¾″ wide.
4. Fold foundation square in quarters; press creases. Fold once again into diagonal quarters; press creases.
5. Beginning on a diagonal crease, position folded strip, having folded edge on crease and strip extending from center to outside corner. Roughly trim excess. Block will be recut later with a rotary cutter. Secure.
6. Overlap folded strip, placing it evenly between previous strip and next fold. Folded edges should face the same direction and strip should extend from center to outside edge, making stripes. To match, you may need to trim excess on both ends.
7. Continue overlapping folded strips around foundation, matching stripes and roughly trimming away excess. When you have covered half of the foundation, you will need to tuck in excess strip under previous strip in center. Trim so you are not tucking in too much fabric. Use an awl or long pin to help tuck fabric under. Save all strips that do not "match." You may be able to use them later as spiral moves around foundation.
8. Carefully tuck under and secure final strip. Notice that the stripes may not match original strip since the spiral has broadened. Minor adjustments can be made to first strip, but an even match is not necessary to achieve spiral effect.
9. Using a machine or hand stitch, tack center securely.
10. Secure around outside edges. Turn potholder to wrong side. Using a rotary cutter and ruler, neatly trim away excess.
11. Baste 2 layers of batting or needlepunch to one side of spiral square. Add backing fabric.
12. Using the technique you prefer, finish raw edges (see pages 7–9).

Mug Rugs

FINISHED SIZE: 3½″ x 3½″ or 4″ x 4″

DIRECTIONS

Any of the 3½″ or 4″ square ornaments can be used under a steaming mug of your favorite beverage. Follow ornament directions on pages 10–17, binding each mug rug with narrow bias binding (minus the hanging loop), fold-over binding, or plain edging that has been topstitched ¼″ away from finished edge (see pages 7–9).

Towel Tops

FINISHED SIZE: approx. 4″ x 25½″

MATERIALS: 45″ wide fabric

4″ x 4″ square: 1 muslin for foundation
4″ x 4″ square: 1 light background fabric
3½″ x 4″ strips: 2 red print #1, 2 green print #1
2½″ x 4″ strips: 2 red print #2, 2 green print #2
1½″ x 4″ strips: 2 red print #3, 2 green print #3
4″ x 4″ square: 1 for backing
1 kitchen hand towel (makes 2)
¼ yd. coordinating print fabric for towel tops
1 large button

DIRECTIONS

1. Assemble Log Cabin ornament according to directions on page 11, but do not bind.
2. Using pattern piece found on page 30, cut towel top and towel top facing from print fabric.
3. With right sides together, stitch folded Log Cabin piece to towel top.
4. With right sides together, stitch towel top to towel top facing in a ¼″ seam, leaving bottom edge open. Turn and press.
5. Cut kitchen towel in half crosswise. Gather top to fit open edge of towel top.
6. With right sides together, stitch towel to front of towel top, leaving facing free. Turn raw edges to inside, turn under seam allowance on facing, and slip-stitch in place.
7. Make buttonhole at top of facing. Stitch button underneath.
8. Towel may be buttoned over towel rack or oven door handle.

Great Gifts

Enlarging these folded fabric designs to 10″ will make the perfect accent for a purse. The 12″ folded fabric squares work well for pillows or a tote bag.

Tote Bag

FINISHED SIZE: 12″ x 12″

MATERIALS: 45″ wide fabric
½ yd. denim or sturdy fabric for tote bag
⅜ yd. coordinating fabric for lining
12½″ x 12½″ Folded Fabric Square (see pages 28–29)

DIRECTIONS

1. Using diagram as a guide, cut fabric for tote bag and lining.

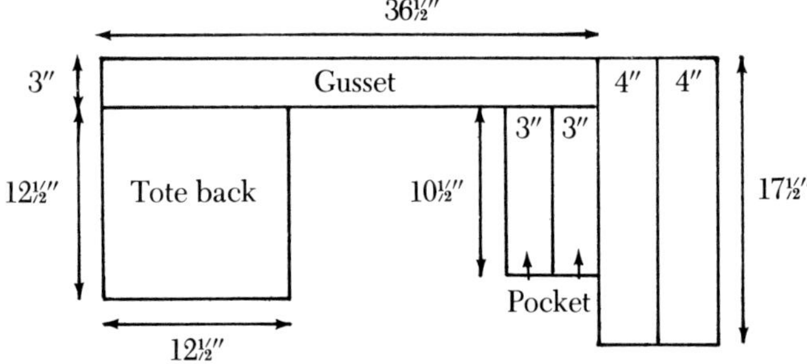

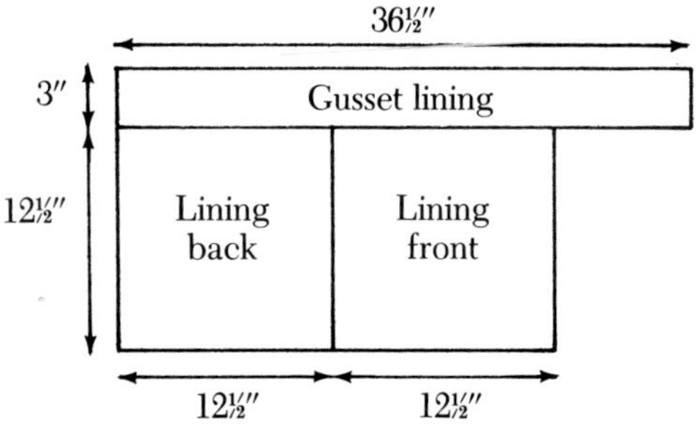

2. Use 12½″ Folded Fabric Square for tote front.
3. Construct gusset with pockets as shown.

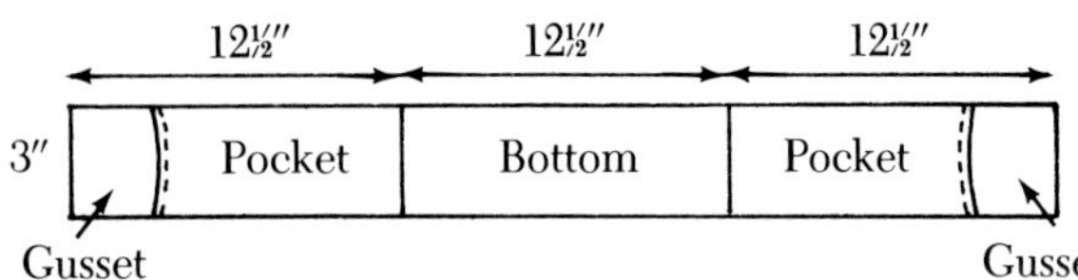

The 12″ Diamond-in-a-Square design makes into a roomy tote bag, while the 10″ Variable Star design accents the flap of a purse.

4. With right sides together, stitch gusset to 12½″ Folded Fabric Square (tote front) and back in a ¼″ seam. Trim corners and turn to outside.
5. To make handles, press each 4½″ x 17½″ piece in half lengthwise with right sides out. Open fabric and fold so that both raw edges are in the middle, resting on the crease you just made; press. Now fold in half lengthwise again, having raw edges on the inside. Stitch close to folded edges. Baste the raw edge of each handle end to the top of the tote front and back, positioning handles 3″ from each edge.
6. Stitch lining sections together in the same manner as the tote front and back, omitting pockets. Place upper edges of lining and tote with right sides together.
7. Stitch around top edges in a ¼″ seam, leaving an opening to turn. (Be careful not to catch in handles.) Turn tote to right side and press to shape. Slip-stitch the opening closed.

Padded Purse

FINISHED SIZE: 10″ x 10″

MATERIALS: 45″ wide fabric
½ yd. fabric for purse, flap backing, and strap
⅜ yd. fabric for lining
10½″ x 10½″ Folded Fabric Square (see pages 26–27)
2″ x 42″ piece of interfacing

DIRECTIONS

1. Cut fabric for purse, flap backing, strap, and lining as shown:

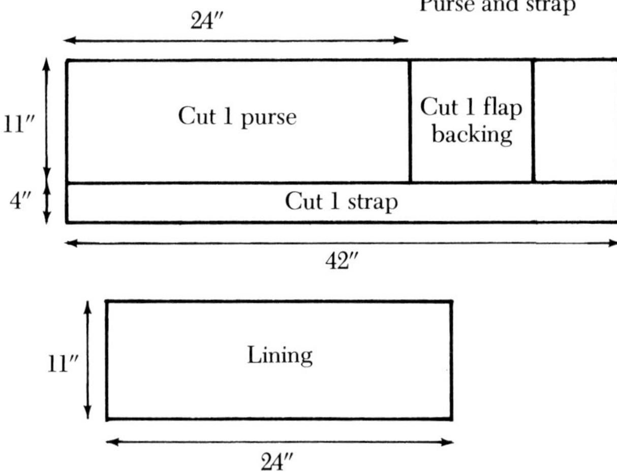

2. Place 10½″ Folded Fabric Square and flap backing piece with right sides together. Stitch in a ¼″ seam along 3 sides. Trim corners and turn to right side; press. Topstitch ¼″ from finished edge. This will be the purse flap.
3. Fold purse with right sides together. Stitch sides in a ¼″ seam. Turn to right side.
4. Pin flap to purse along upper edge, placing fabric square next to right side of fabric. Baste in place.

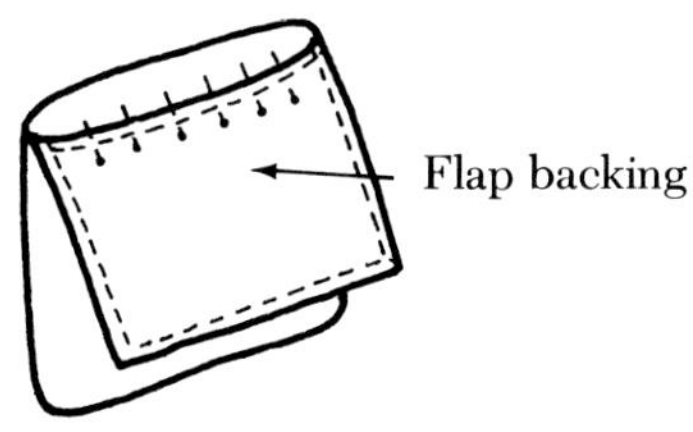

5. Baste interfacing to wrong side of strap. (Note: Interfacing is only ½ width of purse strap.) Fold strap lengthwise with right sides together and stitch in a ¼″ seam. Turn to right side; press. Pin in place on outside of purse, positioning along upper edge at side seams.
6. Fold lining with right sides together. Stitch sides in a ¼″ seam. Do not turn to right side.
7. Slip purse flap section inside of lining and pin together along upper edge. Right side of purse and flap will be next to right side of lining.

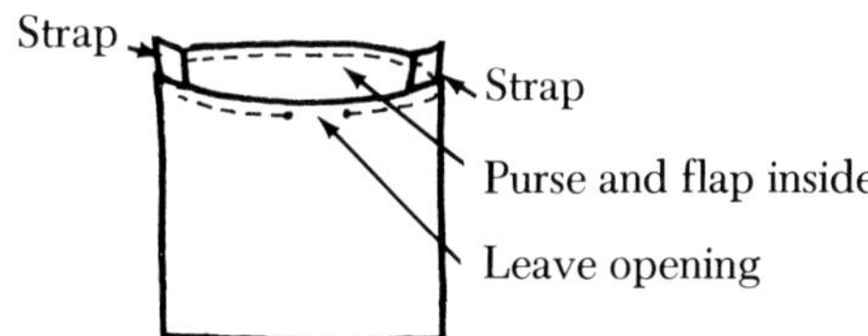

8. Stitch along upper edge of purse through all thicknesses, leaving an opening for turning.
9. Turn purse to right side through opening. Arrange lining to drop down inside of purse. To secure lining and to shape purse sides with a "bottom," fold a small triangle of fabric at each corner. Stitch through all thicknesses.

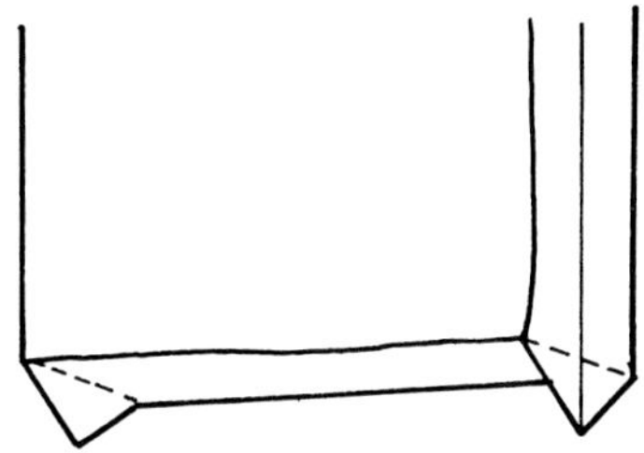

10. Slip-stitch opening closed.

Pillows

FINISHED SIZE: 12″ x 12″

MATERIALS: 45″ wide fabric
⅜ yd. fabric for backing
12½″ x 12½″ Folded Fabric Square (see pages 28–29)
1⅜ yd. cording, piping, or ruffled trim
12″ pillow form

DIRECTIONS

1. Cut a 12½″ x 12½″ square from fabric for backing, or cut 2 pieces 8″ x 12½″ for lapped back.
2. Baste trim to right side of 12½″ Folded Fabric Square, having finished edge of trim toward center of block and raw edges even.
3. With right sides together, pin pillow back to front. Stitch in a ¼″ seam, leaving an opening for turning. Turn and insert pillow form. Slip-stitch opening closed.

Folded fabric designs done in the 12″ size make wonderful pillows. Shown from left to right are: Variable Star, Diamond-in-a-Square, Spiral, and Christmas Cross.

Folded Fabric Squares (10½″)

To make a lapped back, which allows a pillow form to easily slip in and out:

1. Make 2 pillow back pieces. Cut each piece the same width as pillow front. Adjust length to equal half the back length plus 2″. Sew a narrow hem along one long edge of each pillow back piece.
2. Follow the diagram for the correct placement of the pillow pieces.

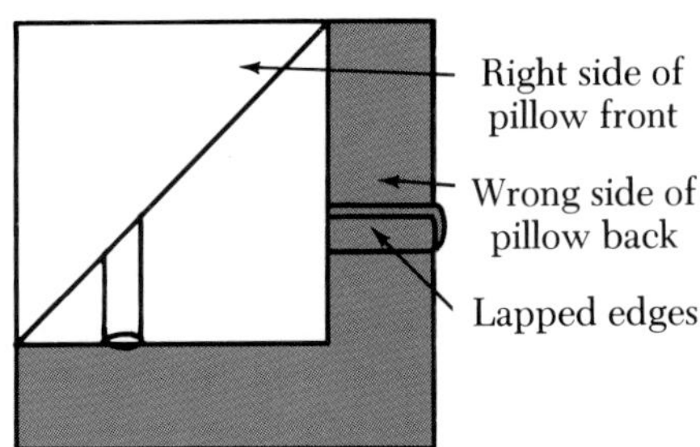

3. Stitch ¼″ from all edges. Trim corners and turn to right side.
4. Insert pillow form.

Variable Star

UNFINISHED SIZE: 10½″ x 10½″

MATERIALS: 45″ wide fabric
½ yd. accent fabric
⅜ yd. white fabric

CUTTING
10½″ x 10½″ square: 1 accent for foundation/star center
8″ x 8″ squares: 4 white for Row 1
5½″ x 10½″ strips: 4 accent for Row 2
5 ½" x 5 ½" squares: 4 white for Row 3
8″ x 8″ squares: 4 white for Row 4

DIRECTIONS
1. See page 12 for construction diagrams.
2. Fold 8″ white squares for Row 1 in half diagonally; press. Position one square in each corner of foundation, having fold toward center and raw edges even along outside edge. Secure along outside edge.
3. Fold accent strips for Row 2 in half lengthwise. (They should measure 2¾″ x 10½″ when folded.) Position one on each side, having fold toward center and raw edges along outside; secure.

4. Fold 5½″ white squares for Row 3 in quarters; press. Position one in each corner, having raw edges even; secure.
5. Fold 8″ white squares for Row 4 in quarters. Position one square along each side, aligning point of square with center diamond; secure. Trim away excess.
6. Using white thread, tack all points of white squares through all layers.

Christmas Cross

UNFINISHED SIZE: 10½″ x10½″

MATERIALS: 45″ wide fabric
½ yd. accent fabric
⅜ yd. white fabric

CUTTING
10½″ x 10½″ square: 1 accent for foundation/star center
8″ x 8″ squares: 4 white for Row 1
5½″ x 10½″ strips: 4 accent for Row 2
5½″ x 5½″ squares: 4 white for Row 3

DIRECTIONS
1. See page 16 for construction diagrams.
2. Fold 8″ white squares for Row 1 in half diagonally; press. Position one square in each corner of foundation, having fold toward center and raw edges even along outside edge. Secure along outside edge.
3. Fold accent strips for Row 2 in half lengthwise. (They should measure 2¾″ x 10½″ when folded.) Position one on each side, having fold toward center and raw edges along outside; secure.
4. Fold 5½″ white squares for Row 3 in quarters; press. Position one in each corner, having raw edges even; secure.
5. Using white thread, tack all points of white squares through all layers.

Diamond-in-a-Square

UNFINISHED SIZE: 10½″ x 10½″

MATERIALS: 45″ wide fabric
⅜ yd. accent fabric
¼ yd. light fabric
¼ yd. medium fabric
¼ yd. dark fabric
¼ yd. white fabric

CUTTING
10½″ x 10½″ square: 1 accent for foundation/center
8″ x 10″ strips: 4 light for Row 1
8″ x 8″ squares: 4 medium for Row 2
5½″ x 10″ strips: 4 dark for Row 3
5½″ x 5½″ squares: 4 white for Row 4

DIRECTIONS
1. See pages 13–14 for construction diagrams.
2. Fold light strips for Row 1 lengthwise; press. Place around outside edge of foundation, having fold toward center and raw edges along outside; secure.
3. Fold medium squares for Row 2 in half diagonally; press. Place in each corner of foundation, having fold toward center and raw edges along outside; secure.
4. Fold dark strips for Row 3 in half lengthwise; press. Position and secure as in Step 1.
5. Fold white squares for Row 4 in half diagonally; press. Position and secure as in Step 2.

Folded Fabric Squares (12½″)

Variable Star

UNFINISHED SIZE: 12½″ x 12½″

MATERIALS: 45″ wide fabric
⅝ yd. accent fabric
¾ yd. white fabric

CUTTING
12½″ x 12½″ square: 1 accent for foundation and star center
9½″ x 9½″ squares: 4 white for Row 1
6½″ x 12½″ strips: 4 accent for Row 2
6½″ x 6½″ squares: 4 white for Row 3
9½″ x 9½″ squares: 4 white for Row 4

DIRECTIONS
1. See page 12 for construction diagrams.
2. Fold 9½″ white squares for Row 1 in half diagonally; press. Position one square in each corner of foundation, having fold toward center and raw edges along outside edge. Secure along outside edge.
3. Fold accent strips for Row 2 in half lengthwise. (They should measure 3¼″ x 12½″ when folded.) Position one on each side, having fold toward center and raw edges along outside; secure.
4. Fold 6½″ white squares for Row 3 in quarters; press. Position one in each corner, having raw edges even; secure.
5. Fold 9½″ white squares for Row 4 in quarters; press. Position one square along each side, aligning point of square with center diamond; secure. Trim away excess.
6. Using white thread, tack all points of white squares through all layers.

Christmas Cross

UNFINISHED SIZE: 12½″ x 12½″

MATERIALS: 45″ wide fabric
⅝ yd. accent fabric
½ yd. white fabric
⅜ yd. fabric for backing (pillow only)

CUTTING
12½″ x 12½″ square: 1 accent for foundation and star center
9½″ x 9½″ squares: 4 white for Row 1
6½″ x 12½″ strips: 4 accent for Row 2
6½″ x 6½″ squares: 4 white for Row 3
12½″ x 12½″ fabric for backing (pillow only)

DIRECTIONS
1. See page 16 for construction diagrams.
2. Fold 9½″ white squares for Row 1 in half diagonally; press. Position one square in each corner of foundation, having fold toward center and raw edges along outside edge. Secure along outside edge.
3. Fold accent strips for Row 2 in half lengthwise. (They should measure 3¼″ x 12½″ when folded.) Position one on each side, having fold toward center and raw edges along outside; secure.
4. Fold white squares for Row 3 in quarters; press. Position one in each corner, having raw edges even; secure.
5. Using white thread, tack all points of white squares through all layers.

Diamond-in-a-Square

UNFINISHED SIZE: 12½″ x 12½″

MATERIALS: 45″ wide fabric
⅜ yd. accent fabric
⅜ yd. light fabric
⅜ yd. medium fabric
⅜ yd. dark fabric
¼ yd. white fabric

CUTTING

12½″ x 12½″ square: 1 accent for foundation and center
9½″ x 12½″ strips: 4 light for Row 1
9½″ x 9½″ squares: 4 medium for Row 2
6½″ x 12½″ strips: 4 dark for Row 3
6½″ x 6½″ squares: 4 white for Row 4

DIRECTIONS

1. See pages 13–14 for construction diagrams.
2. Fold light strips for Row 1 lengthwise; press. Place around outside edge of foundation, having fold toward center and raw edges along outside; secure.
3. Fold medium squares for Row 2 in half diagonally; press. Place in each corner of foundation, having fold toward center and raw edges along outside; secure.
4. Fold dark strips for Row 3 in half lengthwise; press. Position and secure as in Step 1.
5. Fold white squares for Row 4 in half diagonally; press. Position and secure as in Step 2.

Spiral

UNFINISHED SIZE: 12½″ x 12½″

MATERIALS: 45″ wide fabric

⅜ yd. muslin
⅞ yd. crosswise-striped fabric

CUTTING

12½″ x 12½″ square: 1 muslin for foundation
5″ wide crosswise strips: 6 striped fabric for spiral

DIRECTIONS

1. Refer to page 17 for construction diagrams.
2. Fold foundation square in quarters; press creases. Fold once again into diagonal quarters; press creases.
3. Press strips in half lengthwise. You should now have 6 folded strips, each 2½″ wide.
4. Beginning on a diagonal crease, position a folded strip on foundation, having folded edge on crease and strip extending from center to outside corner. Roughly trim excess. Block will be recut later with a rotary cutter; secure.
5. Overlap folded strip (you will need to secure 2 strips between diagonal-line strip and straight-line strip), having folded edges face the same direction and strip extend from center to outside edge. Match stripes on strips, roughly trimming excess at center and outside edges.
6. Continue overlapping folded strips around foundation, matching stripes and roughly trimming away excess. When you have covered half of the foundation, you will need to tuck in excess strip under previous strip in center. Trim so you are not tucking in too much fabric. Use an awl or long pin to help tuck fabric under. Save all strips that do not "match." You may be able to use them later as spiral moves around foundation.
7. Carefully tuck under and secure final strip. Notice that the stripes may not match original strip since the spiral has broadened. Minor adjustments can be made to first strip, but an even match is not necessary to achieve spiral effect.
8. Using a machine or hand stitch, tack center securely. Add a dab of glue behind the longest strips (4 strips going from center to corner) to help stabilize them.
9. Secure square around outside edges; turn to wrong side. Using a rotary cutter and ruler, neatly trim away excess.

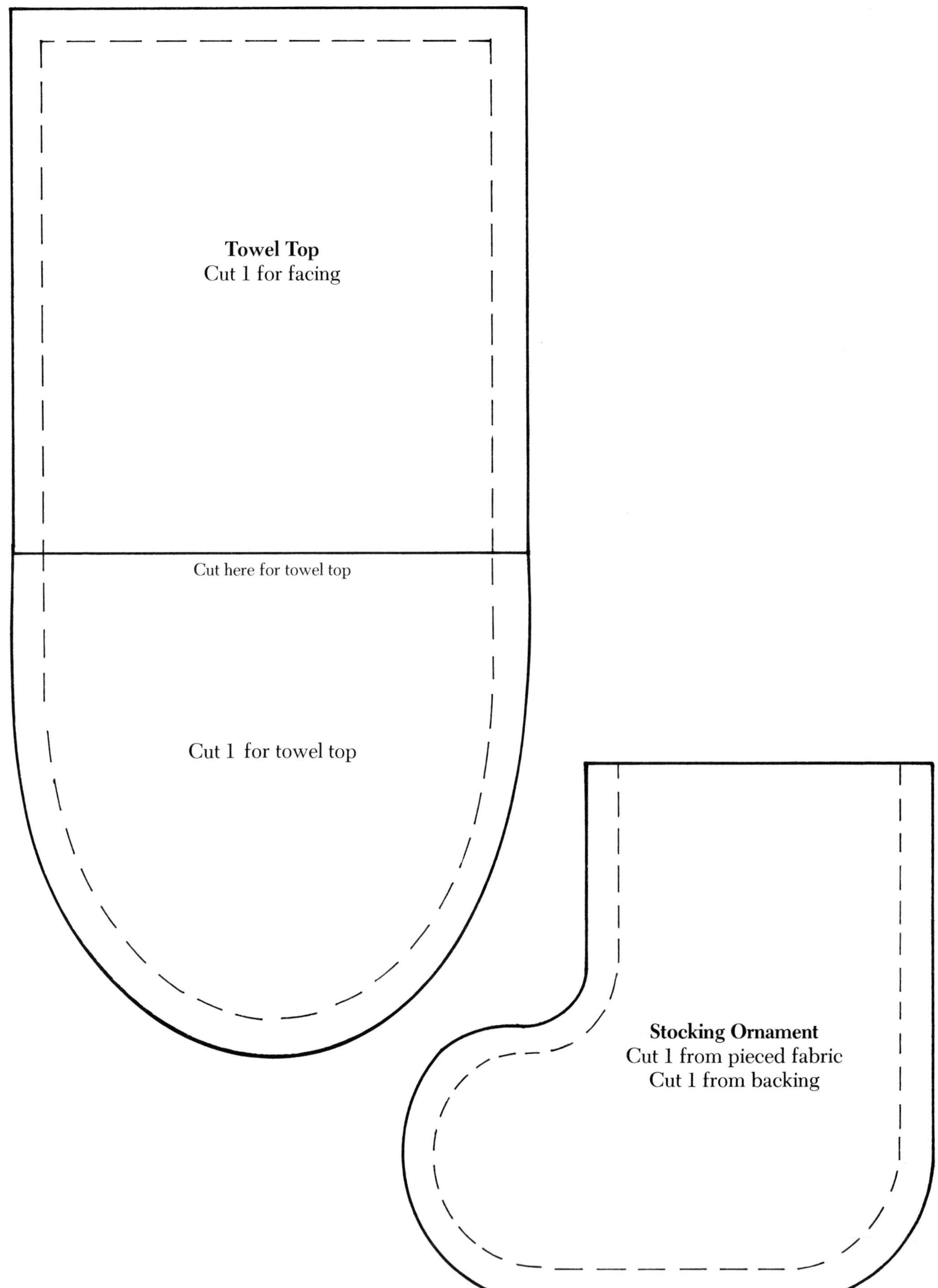
Towel Top
Cut 1 for facing
Cut here for towel top
Cut 1 for towel top
Stocking Ornament
Cut 1 from pieced fabric
Cut 1 from backing

Notes

Other Martingale & Company Publications and Products

THAT PATCHWORK PLACE TITLES:

AMERICA'S BEST-LOVED QUILT BOOKS®

All New Copy Art for Quilters
All-Star Sampler • Roxanne Carter
Appliquilt® • Tonee White
Appliquilt® for Christmas • Tonee White
Appliquilt® to Go • Tonee White
Appliquilt® Your ABCs • Tonee White
Around the Block with Judy Hopkins
At Home with Quilts • Nancy J. Martin
Baltimore Bouquets • Mimi Dietrich
Bargello Quilts • Marge Edie
Beyond Charm Quilts • Catherine L. McIntee & Tammy L. Porath
Bias Square® Miniatures • Christine Carlson
Blockbender Quilts • Margaret J. Miller
Block by Block • Beth Donaldson
Borders by Design • Paulette Peters
The Border Workbook • Janet Kime
Calicoes & Quilts Unlimited • Judy Betts Morrison
The Cat's Meow • Janet Kime
Celebrate! with Little Quilts • Alice Berg, Mary Ellen Von Holt & Sylvia Johnson
Celebrating the Quilt
Class-Act Quilts
Classic Quilts with Precise Foundation Piecing • Tricia Lund & Judy Pollard
Color: The Quilter's Guide • Christine Barnes
Colourwash Quilts • Deirdre Amsden
Crazy but Pieceable • Hollie A. Milne
Crazy Rags • Deborah Brunner
Decorate with Quilts & Collections • Nancy J. Martin
Down the Rotary Road with Judy Hopkins
Dress Daze • Judy Murrah
Dressed by the Best
The Easy Art of Appliqué • Mimi Dietrich & Roxi Eppler
Easy Machine Paper Piecing • Carol Doak
Easy Mix & Match Machine Paper Piecing • Carol Doak
Easy Paper-Pieced Keepsake Quilts • Carol Doak
Easy Reversible Vests • Carol Doak
Easy Seasonal Wall Quilts • Deborah J. Moffett-Hall
A Fine Finish • Cody Mazuran
Five- and Seven-Patch Blocks & Quilts for the ScrapSaver • Judy Hopkins
Four-Patch Blocks & Quilts for the ScrapSaver • Judy Hopkins
Freedom in Design • Mia Rozmyn
From a Quilter's Garden • Gabrielle Swain
Go Wild with Quilts • Margaret Rolfe
Go Wild with Quilts—Again! • Margaret Rolfe
Great Expectations • Karey Bresenhan with Alice Kish & Gay E. McFarland
Hand-Dyed Fabric Made Easy • Adriene Buffington
Happy Endings • Mimi Dietrich
Honoring the Seasons • Takako Onoyama
Jacket Jazz • Judy Murrah
Jacket Jazz Encore • Judy Murrah
The Joy of Quilting • Joan Hanson & Mary Hickey
Kids Can Quilt • Barbara J. Eikmeier
Life in the Country with Country Threads • Mary Tendall & Connie Tesene
Little Quilts • Alice Berg, Mary Ellen Von Holt & Sylvia Johnson
Lively Little Logs • Donna McConnell
Living with Little Quilts • Alice Berg, Mary Ellen Von Holt & Sylvia Johnson
The Log Cabin Design Workbook • Christal Carter
Lora & Company • Lora Rocke
Loving Stitches • Jeana Kimball
Machine Needlelace and Other Embellishment Techniques • Judy Simmons
Machine Quilting Made Easy • Maurine Noble
Magic Base Blocks for Unlimited Quilt Designs • Patty Barney & Cooky Schock
Miniature Baltimore Album Quilts • Jenifer Buechel
Mirror Manipulations • Gail Valentine
More Jazz from Judy Murrah
More Quilts for Baby • Ursula Reikes
More Strip-Pieced Watercolor Magic • Deanna Spingola
Nine-Patch Blocks & Quilts for the ScrapSaver • Judy Hopkins
No Big Deal • Deborah L. White
Once upon a Quilt • Bonnie Kaster & Virginia Athey
Patchwork Pantry • Suzette Halferty & Carol C. Porter
A Perfect Match • Donna Lynn Thomas
A Pioneer Doll and Her Quilts • Mary Hickey
Press for Success • Myrna Giesbrecht
Quilted for Christmas, Book II
Quilted for Christmas, Book III
Quilted for Christmas, Book IV
Quilted Landscapes • Joan Blalock
Quilted Legends of the West • Judy Zehner & Kim Mosher
Quilted Sea Tapestries • Ginny Eckley
A Quilter's Ark • Margaret Rolfe
Quilting Design Sourcebook • Dorothy Osler
Quilting Makes the Quilt • Lee Cleland
Quilting Up a Storm • Lydia Quigley
Quilts: An American Legacy • Mimi Dietrich
Quilts for Baby • Ursula Reikes
Quilts for Red-Letter Days • Janet Kime
Quilts Say It Best • Eileen Westfall
Refrigerator Art Quilts • Jennifer Paulson
Rotary Riot • Judy Hopkins & Nancy J. Martin
Rotary Roundup • Judy Hopkins & Nancy J. Martin
Round Robin Quilts • Pat Magaret & Donna Slusser
Sensational Settings • Joan Hanson
Sew a Work of Art Inside and Out • Charlotte Bird
Shortcuts: A Concise Guide to Rotary Cutting • Donna Lynn Thomas
Show Me How to Paper-Piece • Carol Doak
Simply Scrappy Quilts • Nancy J. Martin
Small Talk • Donna Lynn Thomas
Square Dance • Martha Thompson
Start with Squares • Martha Thompson
Strip-Pieced Watercolor Magic • Deanna Spingola
Stripples • Donna Lynn Thomas
Stripples Strikes Again! • Donna Lynn Thomas
Strips That Sizzle • Margaret J. Miller
Sunbonnet Sue All Through the Year • Sue Linker
Template-Free® Quilts and Borders • Trudie Hughes
Threadplay with Libby Lehman • Libby Lehman
Through the Window & Beyond • Lynne Edwards
The Total Bedroom • Donna Babylon
Traditional Blocks Meet Appliqué • Deborah J. Moffett-Hall
Traditional Quilts with Painless Borders • Sally Schneider & Barbara J. Eikmeier
Transitions • Andrea Balosky
Tropical Punch • Marilyn Dorwart
True Style • Peggy True
Variations in Chenille • Nannette Holmberg
Victorian Elegance • Lezette Thomason
Watercolor Impressions • Pat Magaret & Donna Slusser
Watercolor Quilts • Pat Magaret & Donna Slusser
Weave It! Quilt It! Wear It! • Mary Anne Caplinger
Welcome to the North Pole • Piece O' Cake Designs
Whimsies & Whynots • Mary Lou Weidman
WOW! Wool-on-Wool Folk Art Quilts • Janet Carija Brandt
Your First Quilt Book (or it should be!) • Carol Doak

4", 6", 8" & metric Bias Square® • BiRangle™
Ruby Beholder® • ScrapMaster • Bias Stripper™
Shortcuts to America's Best-Loved Quilts (video)

FIBER STUDIO PRESS TITLES:

FIBER STUDIO PRESS

Complex Cloth • Jane Dunnewold
Dyes & Paints • Elin Noble
Erika Carter: Personal Imagery in Art Quilts • Erika Carter
Fine Art Quilts: Work by Artists of the Contemporary QuiltArt Association
Inspiration Odyssey • Diana Swim Wessel
The Nature of Design • Joan Colvin
Thread Magic • Ellen Anne Eddy
Velda Newman: A Painter's Approach to Quilt Design • Velda Newman with Christine Barnes

Many titles are available at your local quilt shop. For more information, write for a free color catalog to Martingale & Company, PO Box 118, Bothell, WA 98041-0118 USA.

☎ U.S. and Canada, call **1-800-426-3126** for the name and location of the quilt shop nearest you.
Int'l: 1-425-483-3313 **Fax:** 1-425-486-7596
E-mail: info@patchwork.com
Web: www.patchwork.com

12.97